THE ART OF

MAFIA III

THE ART OF

MAFIA III

TITAN BOOKS

An Insight Editons Book

CONTENTS

INTRODUCTION

Slowly staggering down a party-heavy street in the French Quarter. Blasting through the bayou in a 1968 American muscle car listening to Dusty Springfield. It's never easy to create a new game world, but how do you do that with an iconic city based on New Orleans during such a turbulent time—the Deep South in the summer of 1968? That's the challenge we gave ourselves for *Mafia III*.

Obviously, there's the architecture of New Bordeaux. We scoured every source we could for archival imagery and footage and scouted locations in Louisiana, both on foot and online, shooting and gathering tons of references to both the time and the place. We looked to classic 1968 movies, books, magazines, newspapers, fashions, and music. Oh man, the music! *Days* have gone by with headphones on, and I could jump into a Lassiter Mogul near General's Circle, pull over to the side, and just listen to the in-game radio station play.

We needed New Bordeaux to feel alive and to seem unique and familiar, even though you'll never set foot there. Since *Mafia III* exists in our own alternate version of 1968 America, we tread a line between the needs of the game, the story, and the importance of remaining true to the events of the time. Ultimately, *Mafia III* is a work of fiction, but I hope it is also enough of a reflection of our real world to ensure that people familiar with the area—and era—will come along for the ride.

Welcome to New Bordeaux.

—**DAVE SMITH**, *Mafia III* Art Director, 2016

SECTION 1
NEW BORDEAUX

If Lincoln Clay is the main character of *Mafia III*, the city of New Bordeaux—based largely on New Orleans—is a close second. The design team's goal was to distill the essence of that great city into a place that would feel familiar and authentic to those who know it well, and approachable and understandable to those who don't.

New Bordeaux is steeped in history. It's a port city with humble beginnings in the docks and markets of River Row, growing as huge ships brought imported goods via Tickfaw Harbor docks. As the game begins, the city is in the process of rebuilding and expanding its downtown. Layers of history, from the 1800s through the 1960s, provide a broad palette from which to draw the game's designs.

Meanwhile, the Mafia has increased in power, with Sal Marcano reaching out into every aspect of the city: vice, politics, commerce, and local communities. Nothing seems beyond his reach, and beneath the old-world facade, the city is hurting as the mob's stranglehold intensifies.

From the historic French Ward to the brand new high-rises, downtown New Bordeaux is a city of contrasts: new and old, progress and heritage. Looking closer, though, the Mafia's influence can be seen everywhere; it controls everything from vice to construction.

Part of creating the character of New Bordeaux was deciding what created the right resonance with the audience. Most important: How can we quickly and clearly communicate the feel of this city? Deciding on the right visual landmarks early in the process helped the team enormously.

Iconic visuals such as the characteristic skyline and the riverboat help draw in the audience. As each of the districts in New Bordeaux has its own character, it's important to reinforce the overall picture of the city from time to time.

At the top of the Mafia criminal empire is Sal Marcano.
Everything that happens in New Bordeaux eventually leads
back to Sal.

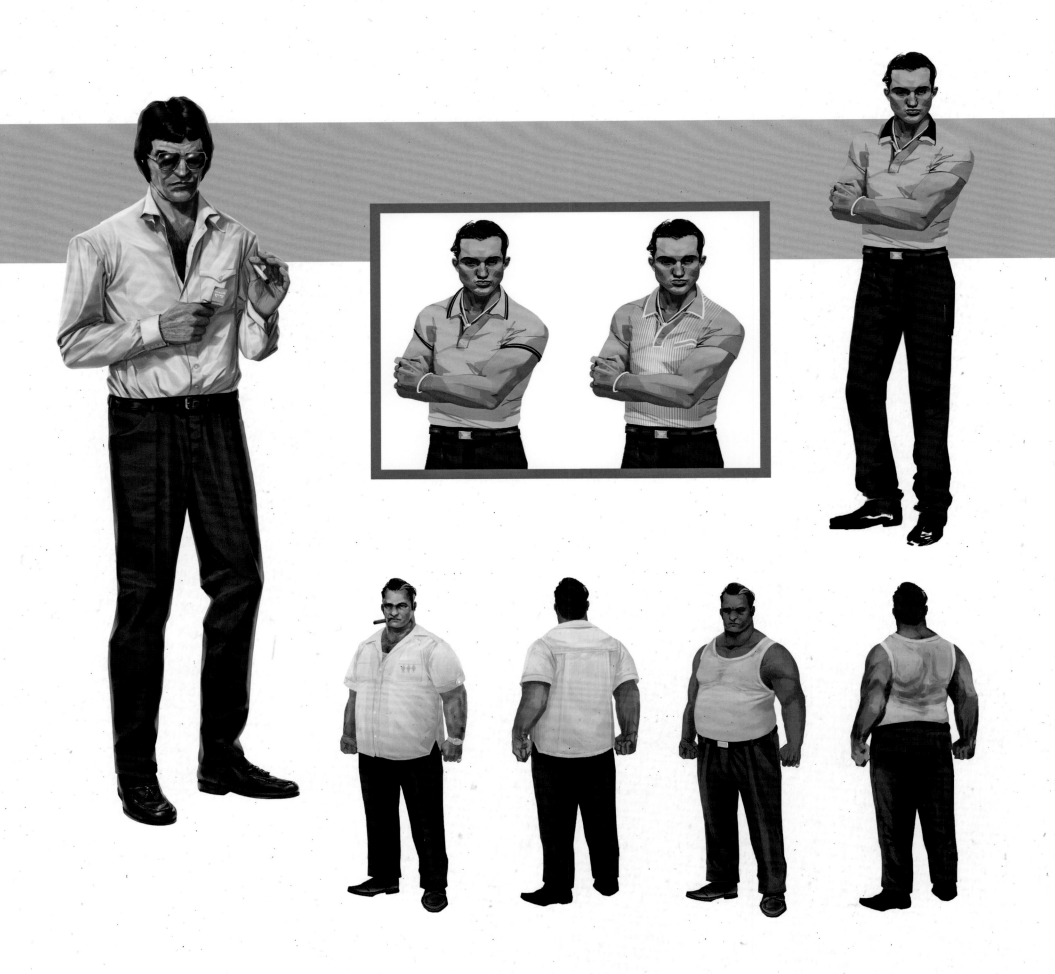

16

At street level, thugs, triggermen, and brutes carry out Sal's will. In designing the appearance of the Mafia goons, the look was kept very late '50s–early '60s to suggest that the Italian mob is something of an anachronism.

Controlling the color palette and keeping the Mafia mostly monochromatic helped pull members out of the crowd and give them their own identity. Strong silhouette design differentiated the various enemy types, from low-level punks with switchblades all the way to the imposing enforcers.

BOURBON CITY
POLICE DEPT
GIORGI MARCANO
67530

For Sal's son, Giorgi Marcano, it was important to stand out from the other Mafia members. Giorgi seems like a flamboyant, hard-drinking, rich kid at first glance, but beneath all the flash, he's a very dangerous character.

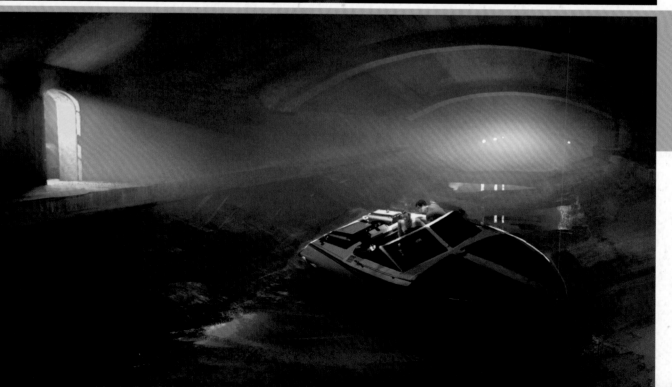

Money makes the world of *Mafia III* go around. And what is the best place to get money fast? The Federal Reserve, of course. Designing the setup for this audacious heist meant depicting beautiful architecture, massive destruction, and, of course, a high-speed chase.

Vice is the Mafia's bread and butter, and no place exemplifies this better than the Paradiso, the culmination of Sal's ambitions in New Bordeaux. All the money ends up here, one way or another.

SECTION 2
DELRAY HOLLOW

Founded in the late 1800s, Delray Hollow has always been a predominantly black district. It has never been a wealthy area, with most of its residents working as sharecroppers, factory workers, or in the canneries.

When Sammy Robinson "took over" Delray Hollow, it was a boom time. He was always careful not to take too much or make anyone feel like they were being exploited.

In 1968, however, money is tighter than ever, and the mob is taking over local community centers and forcing businesses out. The Haitian gangs are pushing back, trying to carve out a slice of the action for themselves. And caught in the middle are Sammy and his crew.

Delray Hollow was inspired by the Algiers neighborhood of New Orleans. In the game, it's one of the oldest districts in the city, with locations stretching back to the turn of the century. Shotgun houses are prevalent here, and the aesthetic combines early twentieth-century wooden structures with the mid-century design seen in motels and other businesses. It's a real melting pot of styles and influences; perfect for the neighborhood in which Lincoln Clay grew up.

Lincoln went to Vietnam in 1966. While serving in a Special Forces unit, he discovered who he truly was. Choosing to wear a field jacket after his tour—as well as his general look—is about him gearing up for war against the Italian Mafia.

Sammy Robinson was Lincoln's surrogate father for many years prior to the younger man's tour in Vietnam. Famous in Delray Hollow for its liquor and music, Sammy's bar is Lincoln's home—something the Italian mob knows all too well.

It was important that Sammy's crew felt new and fashionable in 1968. Its design is at the crossroads of sharp suits and black leather—MLK meets Black Panthers, with a dash of jazz and blues.

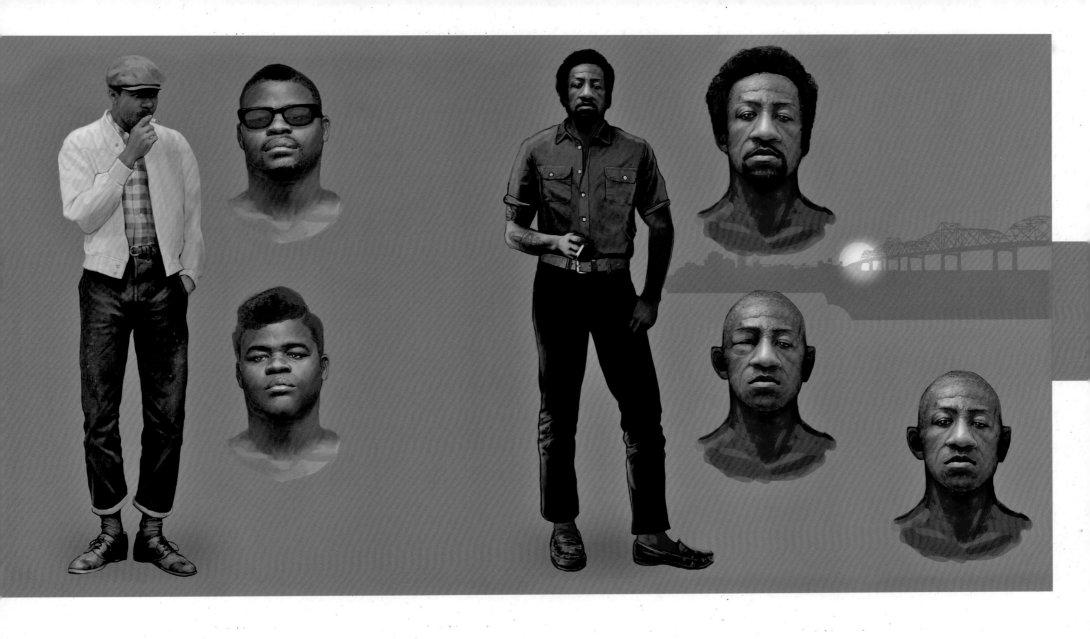

The Pierced Heart Voodoo Shop is a hub for the poor of Delray Hollow. It is designed to present a façade to the public to conceal its ties to the mob—tourist trap out front, smuggling and dirty money in the back.

CASSANDRA

Cassandra went through a lot of revisions before the designers settled on her final look. Her background and motivations changed over the course of development and, indeed, throughout the game itself. Plus, she's not who she seems to be at first glance.

The Mafia is starving Delray Hollow financially while seizing control of beloved local community centers. Sammy's ambitions for the refurbishment of this church have been put permanently on hold now that the mob has taken control.

An amusement park left to rot and decay is yet another symbol of the Mafia's creeping influence in Delray Hollow. Built in the 1930s and '40s, the park was designed for the African-American community, and just before it was completed, the funding was pulled. Now, it's a no-man's-land.

In the absence of money, nature and decay have taken over. One of the biggest creative challenges of the game was telling the story of the park through layers of decaying design history: when and why the park was built; how the style changed over the past thirty years; how the park is used and perceived in gameplay.

One of Lincoln's biggest allies is Donovan, his former CIA handler from Vietnam. Donovan's hotel room—which serves as his war room—has a constant pall of cigarette smoke and filth. This is a man who doesn't care about impressing anyone. In fact, he loves pushing people's buttons.

SECTION 3
POINTE VERDUN

Pointe Verdun, one of the oldest neighborhoods in New Bordeaux, was formed by French colonists shortly after the city's founding. As the city grew, the original settlers relocated to more desirable locations and were replaced by immigrants. In the early 1900s, the Irish settled into the area, and their influence remains.

The neighborhood is solidly lower-working class, and most of its residents work in the nearby shipyard or in other parts of the city where manual labor is required.

Pointe Verdun is home to Thomas Burke and his gang, thieves and car-racers who operate out of his scrapyard-turned-chop shop.

The district contains a wide variety of styles: Junkyards, warehouses, and light industry sit alongside markets, grand churches, and the picturesque lakeshore to the north. And, this being the place that the Tickfaw Harbor workers come home to every night, it also hosts a lot of bars.

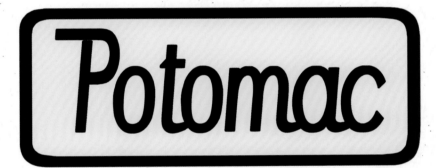

Pointe Verdun is a commercial district, but it's also the blue-collar, low-income area where many of the Irish and dockworkers make their homes. Scrapyards, ironwork shops, and rusting water towers are a big part of the landscape. It's also where one of Lincoln's old friends, Danny Burke, hails from.

Thomas Burke is a train wreck of a man who took creativity to design. He needed to look a little ridiculous without undermining his more serious moments. The paisley shirt was the key; once that was locked in, everything else seemed to fall into place.

IRISH BOSS

IRISH BOSS

One underlying theme throughout the game is that many businesses in New Bordeaux have two sides: what the public sees and what really happens behind the scenes. The meat-packing plant, in particular, is a pretty nasty operation. It's another example of the Mafia subverting the city to their own ends.

The Sweetwater Distillery is firmly in the grip of the Mafia; booze is just another way of putting the squeeze on the locals and keeping the money flooding in. There are lots of interesting textures and materials in this building that give it a unique feel.

SECTION 4
RIVER ROW

From the time of the city's founding through the 1930s, River Row served as the primary port of call for the entire city. Every ship entering and leaving "Bourbon City," the colloquial name for New Bordeaux, went through River Row, which made it a very lucrative area for the mob.

That all changed with World War II. The Navy needed hundreds of ships constructed in a short amount of time, so a new shipyard was constructed in the northeastern part of the city. When it opened in 1943, Tickfaw Harbor immediately dwarfed River Row; within a few months, the only vessels mooring at River Row were small fishing boats. There are still a handful of smaller canneries operating in the area, but most of them closed as business moved to the new shipyard.

Inevitably, the harbor features a lot of early twentieth-century wooden and brick structures. River Row is a district firmly in decline. It's here that we find Vito Scaletta, formerly of Empire Bay, now eking out a miserable existence with the remnants of his Mafia gang.

Vito, the hero of *Mafia II*, is no longer welcome in Empire Bay. Thanks to a few strings that got pulled by Leo Gallante, he wound up in New Bordeaux where he's equally unwelcome. Over the past sixteen years, he's been squeezed until he's working out of a crappy rundown office above a crappy rundown restaurant in the crappiest part of River Row. This is just one of his motivations for joining up with Lincoln Clay.

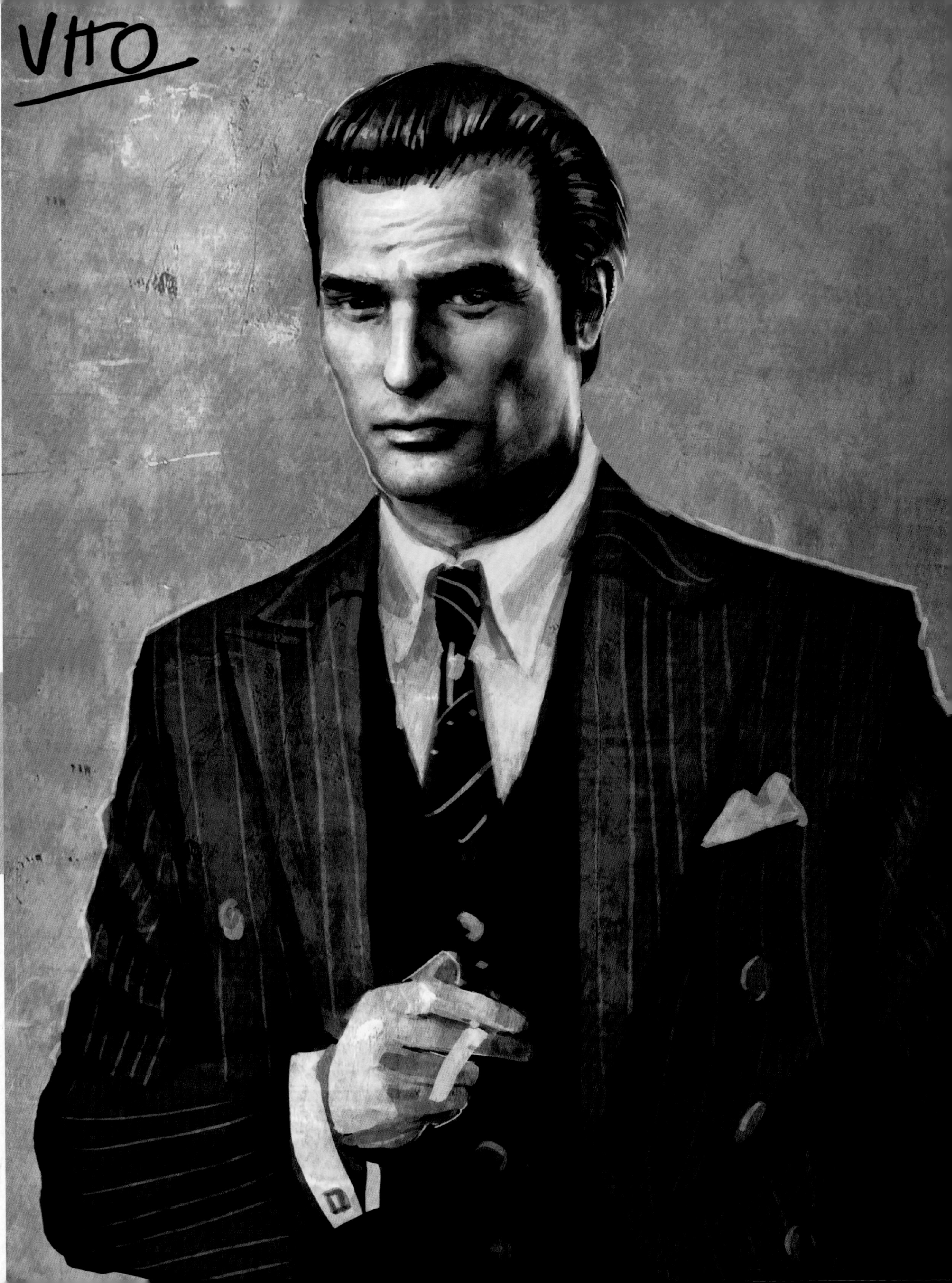
VITO

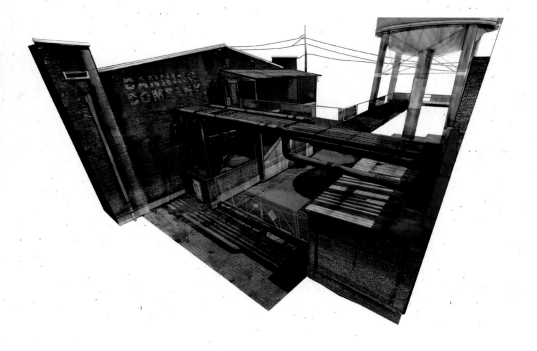

The dockworkers are now controlled by the Mafia, and nobody works unless the mob gets their cut. This part of the city is corrupt from top to bottom. The Mafia has a stranglehold on the docks—it's one of the mob-run rackets at work in this part of New Bordeaux.

STRIKE!

AGAINST
LOW WAGES

DOCK
WORKERS
UNITE

SUPPORT YOUR LOCAL
DOCK UNION

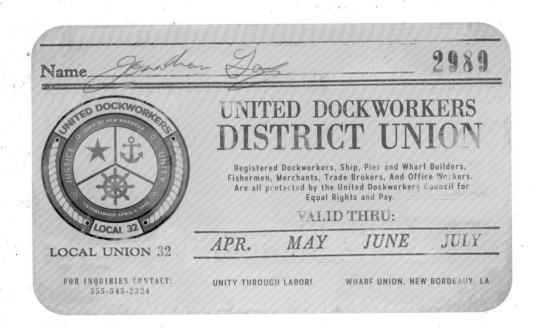

Name *Jonathan Day*   2989

UNITED DOCKWORKERS
DISTRICT UNION

Registered Dockworkers, Ship, Pier and Wharf Builders,
Fishermen, Merchants, Trade Brokers, And Office Workers.
Are all protected by the United Dockworkers Council for
Equal Rights and Pay.

VALID THRU:

APR.   MAY   JUNE   JULY

LOCAL UNION 32

FOR INQUIRIES CONTACT: UNITY THROUGH LABOR!   WHARF UNION, NEW BORDEAUX, LA
555-545-2324

Here's one more example of the rot settling into the New Bordeaux underworld. For the longest time, the Mafia avoided getting involved in the drug trade. But as Sal puts the squeeze on others, they need to find new ways to bring in money—like having a warehouse operate as a front for marijuana distribution.

SECTION 5
DOWNTOWN & FRENCH WARD

These two districts are the heart of New Bordeaux, and along with the bayou, form the visual backbone of the city. The whole history of the city is represented here, from nineteenth-century buildings dotted throughout the French Ward to the brand-new modernist high-rises of downtown.

Layers and layers of history built up over more than a century breathe life into New Bordeaux. From the beginning of development, it was hugely important that the city feel like it had a history beyond the specific game events of 1968.

It's here that people new to New Bordeaux—and to New Orleans, for that matter—can get a feel for the mood, look, and time period of the city and the game. It's a distillation of life in New Bordeaux designed to be accessible, aspirational, and recognizable for new players.

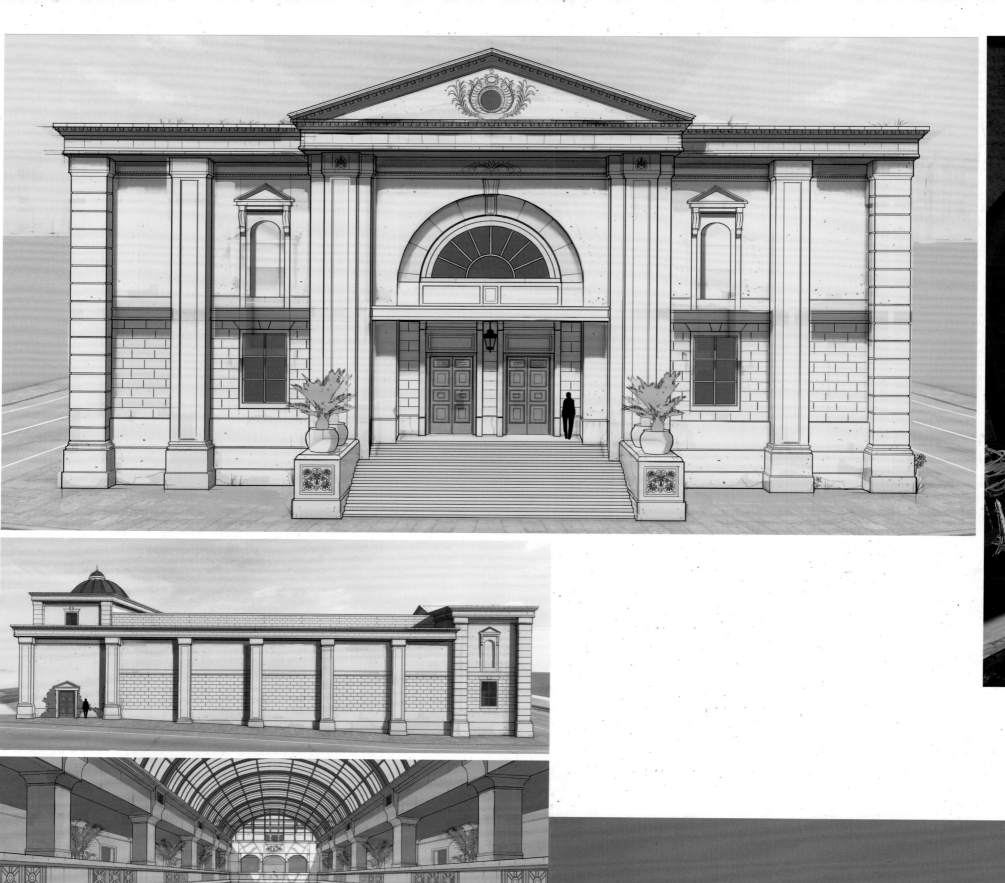
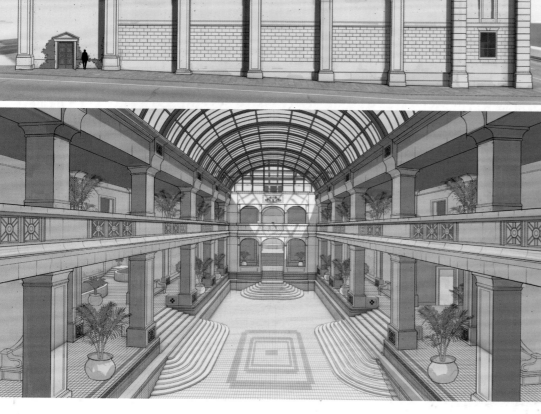

For Made Men, the Bathhouse is a safe place to talk business and make deals. Neoclassical architectural stylings and a whole lot of dubious taste in furnishings make this place the epitome of old-school Italian Mafia excess.

Downtown and the French Ward have two different vibes, but they both revolve around a very similar theme: vice. There's a sense of excess everywhere, whether it's extortion and bribing city officials or strip clubs and drugs.

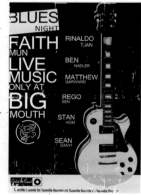

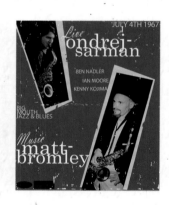

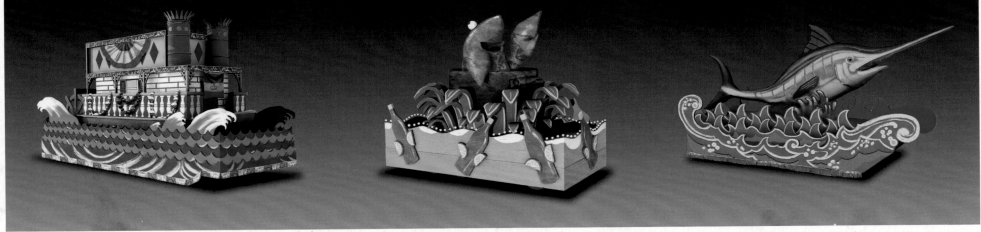

Only a short walk off the main streets of the French Ward is a very different side of the city. Just behind the old-world charm, armed Mafiosi are shaking down the locals, pushing drugs and prostitution.

The Royal Hotel is a symbol of change in downtown New Bordeaux. One of the first high-rise buildings to be built, it's a modernist symbol of wealth and power. It's no surprise that the Mafia is here, preying on the rich and influential.

Hidden behind a more respectable façade is a bordello for the wealthy and powerful of New Bordeaux. A unique combination of glamor and squalor, it caters to the elite's most unusual tastes.

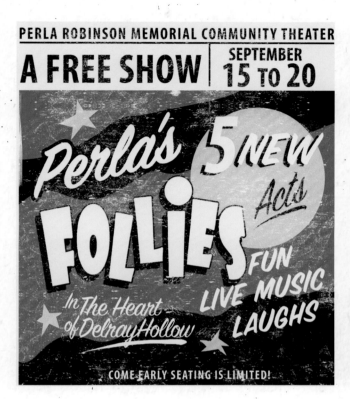

It was important to continually reinforce time and place through architecture and set dressings that ooze late '60s style. This was also an opportunity to weave together the narratives of different locations in the city and make everything feel connected.

In the theme of things getting repurposed in New Bordeaux, this club was originally owned by Sammy—and named in honor of his wife. It came across as a classy operation. Over time, it has changed into a pseudo-legitimate strip club on the surface, but it is really something much worse. It's probably one of the darker corners of the game.

ALLEY CAT

JUNGLE

SECTION 6
BARCLAY MILLS & FRISCO FIELDS

Barclay Mills is the industrial hub of New Bordeaux. Heavy industry, mining, and waste processing all have a home here.

Visually, this gave us an amazing opportunity to present some very different spaces: for example, the wide-open, dusty quarry with an almost old-West feel and the garbage dump with its towers of trash and toxic waste stores.

And, of course, everywhere you turn, the Mafia is there. They influence every industry and control the flow of money and supplies to the rest of the city.

Frisco Fields is where the elite of the city live and do business. Sheltered away in an exclusive community with private security guards, it's a place that Lincoln cannot enter unnoticed.

This is the suburban American dream of the 1950s starting to show cracks in its previously perfect facade. Elite clubs, a prestigious college—nothing is untainted by the mob's actions.

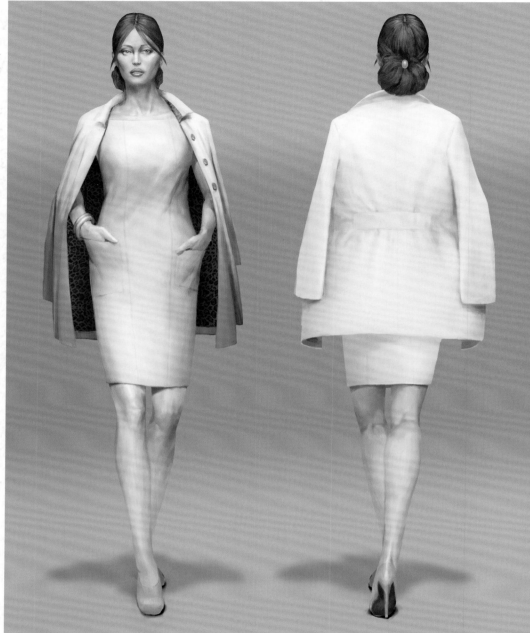

Olivia Marcano, Sal's sister, uses her influence among the city's elite to further her family's criminal enterprises. Olivia's design utilizes the palette established for the family as a whole. Always surrounded by wealth, she holds court in an exclusive yacht club in Frisco Fields.

Blue-collar and white-collar collide in New Bordeaux. Where Barclay Mills butts up against Frisco Fields, you have an impoverished, industrial part of the city with a clear view of all the modern architecture and affluence cropping up just north in Frisco Fields. This causes some of the obvious social tension happening throughout the city.

Run-down areas were originally interjected into the wealthiest parts of town to provide some immediate contrast. Some of this ended up being too much of a tonal shift for a place like Frisco Fields, but a few elements remain in the final game.

Not even the garbage dump can escape the Mafia's grip. This location was an opportunity to push some unique textures and materials: huge piles of trash, industrial machinery, and a layout that encourages a variety of play styles.

High up in the hills of Barclay Mills is a quarry that feeds the city's construction industry. Things have slowed to a crawl in recent years because of the Mafia's control of unions and construction contracts. This setting was a perfect backdrop for an old-fashioned shoot-out.

SECTION 7
TICKFAW HARBOR & SOUTHDOWNS

Once an underdeveloped patch of swampland, Tickfaw Harbor saw big renovations throughout World War II as it became a major port of call for the military. Once the war came to an end, those in organized crime stepped in and renovated the harbor area with the latest shipping equipment.

Over the course of the next several years, Tickfaw Harbor rendered River Row obsolete, becoming one of the largest shipping hubs in the United States. Now the mob uses it to run illegal goods into the country, controlling shipping and warehousing across the district.

Southdowns is a humble, solidly middle-class district and, generally speaking, our most traditional Italian mob neighborhood. It operates as a blue-collar counter to the wealthy community of Frisco Fields. Residents of Southdowns consider themselves to be respectable, hard-working individuals who simply want to take care of their families.

Southdowns is where many low-level and retired mobsters reside. This is a well-known fact throughout the city, and because of that, crime is nonexistent—at least those crimes that the resident mobsters aren't behind. The people who live in Southdowns are devout Catholics who've had to fight, claw, and probably kill for everything they have. There's a general distrust of anyone not from the district and especially minorities.

The Mafia smuggles in goods from abroad, and Tickfaw Harbor is where the biggest shipments arrive. Tickfaw really shows the evolution of the city, maintaining 1920s docks next to huge warehouses and modern ships.

Southdowns is home to the lower- to middle-class residents of New Bordeaux as well as a couple of unsanctioned boxing matches and gambling events, which happen behind closed doors. The Acadia is a prime example of how the Marcano family operates at the fringes of the law.

SECTION 8
BAYOU FANTOM

The bayou is a large unincorporated area to the south of the city.
Because of its isolation, it is home to a wide array of semi-hidden
criminal activities, such as moonshining and drug smuggling.
The Italian mob has little to no direct presence here, preferring to
conduct its business within New Bordeaux.

The bayou is divided up into several distinct visual areas,
balancing navigational ease with the feeling that one could get lost
in it. There are abandoned plantation houses, small towns, trailer
parks, an old oil refinery, and countless unmarked areas to explore
and discover.

It's an ideal place for Lincoln to use as a staging area; as
his family grows, the anonymity afforded by Bayou Fantom's
geography allows him to organize in secret. However, there are
plenty of folks out in the swamps who don't want anyone snooping
around their business. The bayou is nothing if not dangerous.

No one really controls the bayous. They are the badlands. It is pure nature: It doesn't care about who comes and goes. It's where the bodies are buried—or eaten by alligators. We wanted it to feel like you could take one wrong turn and get lost. You'll find Dixie and Haitian gangs, old shipwrecks, and dilapidated plantations, as well as places to tear through the bayou in your car. It's our opportunity to have more fun with the world and for you to just explore.

Radev distillery - Adrien Girod
2013

When laying out the bayou, we developed many ideas for landmarks to help orient the player in this wilderness. The bayou is littered throughout with locations like this abandoned church.

The Haitian camp is the remnant of a village built around a salt mine. It utilizes traditional Haitian voodoo imagery and patterns, rich colors, and intricate designs for the set dressing. This is not the commercialized voodoo sold to the tourists but the real religion.

The church needed to be the focal point for the level, just as it is for the Haitians. Composition and lighting, coupled with selective use of the Haitians' bold palette, lead the player through the mission to this beautiful building.

Earth tones combined with red accents drive the look of the Haitians. Several color palettes were explored—some too stereotypical—before this look, which made sense next to the Dixie mob's shared materials like cotton and leather, was settled on. The Haitians' aesthetic has a slimmer silhouette and warmer palette than the design of the Dixie mob.

Way down at the southern tip of the bayou is an old lighthouse. No one knows why the mob is out there, but at night, there's a lot of activity. The lighthouse uses a very muted color palette, relying on reddish rooftops and selective lighting to help orient the player.

Lincoln meets with his lieutenants at key moments in the game to decide power allocations and future plans. An abandoned plantation house is his choice for the meet-up location. Buried deep in the bayou, it's hidden from the eyes of the police and the mob.

Lou Marcano's riverboat is his pride and joy, bringing him old-world luxury on the water. Dark polished wood and rich décor are keys to the look of the interior, with its bars, casinos, and theater catering to the whims of New Bordeaux high society.

"Uncle" Lou Marcano runs vice in New Bordeaux for his brother, Sal. His design evolved over time from a more buffoonish character to a guy who is a power broker and influencer among the city's most affluent citizens.

Lincoln sends a message to Sal: "I will burn what is yours." This sequence is one of the most complex and exciting in the game—gunplay, fire, explosions, and a visual nod to Lincoln's experiences in Vietnam.

SECTION 9
EMPIRE BAY

As we developed New Bordeaux, we wanted to ensure that *Mafia III* connected strongly with the franchise heritage. As the setting for *Mafia II*, Empire Bay provided a jumping-off point from which to develop an in-game version of the 1960s. Developers investigated how Empire Bay itself would change and how the world would develop during the fifteen-year gap between the two games. A lot of Empire Bay assets were leveraged in early explorations of New Bordeaux, before being replaced with final designs.

Though Empire Bay isn't the location of *Mafia III*, its presence is still felt. *Mafia III* characters grew up there, and the Mafia itself is connected across cities. Empire Bay is still very much a thriving metropolis in the game's 1968, and the observant player will see its influence on New Bordeaux from time to time.

Some of the ideas for New Bordeaux developed in a different city entirely, including the amusement park and diner designs. Developers took Empire Bay forward fifteen years from the end of *Mafia II* to figure out how a very different southern city like New Bordeaux would look. It was an exercise in contrast.

Some early images of the property development that ended up dominating the look of the downtown district: Grand interiors and towering high-rise concrete buildings overtook the older, rundown parts of New Bordeaux.

The construction racket, designed with Empire Bay in mind, was ultimately transplanted to New Bordeaux.

SECTION 10
CHARACTER GALLERY

There are thousands of characters in an open-world game such as *Mafia III*. Collected here are a few of the designs for some of the more interesting and unusual characters Lincoln encounters on his journey to get to Sal.

Each of these characters goes through many revisions, and none is designed in isolation. *Mafia III* is an ensemble piece, and every character needs its own design space to be able to visually communicate its personality and backstory while fitting in with narrative and gameplay requirements.

Early ideas for some of Lincoln's contacts and allies. All are deliberately pushed away from the classic mobster look, either with obvious silhouette and wardrobe choices or more subtly in the specific tailoring of a suit.

NICKY

An example of a character whose early designs are unrecognizable is Nicki, Burke's car-racing daughter, who started life as a lounge singer. As the story matured and the characters started to find their place, Nicki was changed to become one of Lincoln's closest friends and allies.

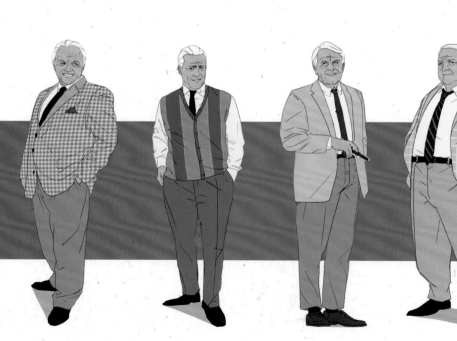

These characters serve as a rogues' gallery of the unsavory types found throughout the city: a butcher, a corrupt judge, an assassin, and an informant. They are proof that the Mafia isn't the only threat facing Lincoln on his quest for vengeance.

MICHAEL

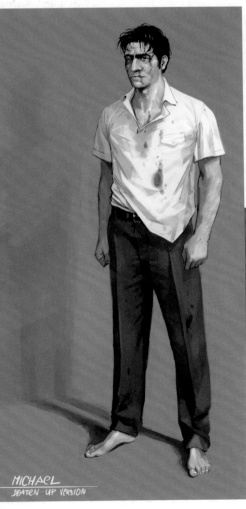

MICHAEL
BEATEN-UP VERSION

TITAN
BOOKS

A division of Titan Publishing Group Ltd
144 Southwark Street, London SE1 0UP
www.titanbooks.com

Find us on Facebook: www.facebook.com/titanbooks
Follow us on Twitter: @TitanBooks

A CIP catalogue record for this title is available from the British Library.

ISBN: 9781785655319

Published by arrangement with Insight Editions, PO Box 3088, San Rafael, CA 94912, USA.
www.insighteditions.com

Publisher: Raoul Goff
Acquisitions Manager: Steve Jones
Art Director: Chrissy Kwasnik
Designer: Brie Brewer
Executive Editor: Vanessa Lopez
Associate Editor: Katie DeSandro
Production Editor: Rachel Anderson
Production Managers: Thomas Chung, Alix Nicholaeff, and Lina sp Temena
Production Assistant: Jacob Frink
Editorial Assistant: Warren Buchanan

ROOTS of PEACE   REPLANTED PAPER

Insight Editions, in association with Roots of Peace, will plant two trees for each tree used in the manufacturing of this book. Roots of Peace is an internationally renowned humanitarian organization dedicated to eradicating land mines worldwide and converting war-torn lands into productive farms and wildlife habitats. Roots of Peace will plant two million fruit and nut trees in Afghanistan and provide farmers there with the skills and support necessary for sustainable land use.

Manufactured in China by Insight Editions

10 9 8 7 6 5 4 3 2 1